Info Product Creation Strategies

Discover How To Make TONS Of Money On Great Demand Selling Information!

**from the library of the
New Thrive Learning Institute**

Get Related Materials

from Our Free Library

Instant Access – Join Here

Click or type into your browser:

http://livesensical.com/go/byob/

LEGAL NOTICE

Table of Contents

Chapter 1: Wealth Goes to the One with the Timeliest Information...4

1.1 Why Sell Information Online?...............................4

1.2 The Single Most Important Kind of Information You Should Sell..5

1.3 A Variety of Information Types You Can Sell Online..6

Chapter 2: First Step to Info Product Creation Strategies...10

2.1 Begin Your Info Product Creation Journey with the End in Mind..10

2.2 The Art of Creating Information on Demand.......11

2.3 Info Product Creation Success Factors................13

Chapter 3: Creating Info Products on the Fly!...15

3.1 Types of Info Products You Can Create.................15

3.2 Churning Out In-Demand Info Products in a Zap 16

3.3 The Elements of a Top Quality Info Product........18

3.4 Branding Your Info Product.................................20

3.5 Getting Your Product's Digital Cover...................22

Chapter 4: Applying the Finishing Touches......24

4.1 How to Protect the Value of Your Info Product....24

4.2 Determining Your Info Product's Terms of Use...25

Chapter 5: Entering Your Info Product into the Market War Zone...27

5.1 How to Strategically Price Your Product...............27

5.2 How to Gather Testimonials for Your Product.....29

5.3 Writing Your Sales Letter....................................30

5.4 Don't Get into Business without Back-End Products!...33

Chapter 6: In Closing.......................................35

6.1 A Crash Course Guide on Marketing to Your Prospects...35

6.2 School of Thought: Go as High-Ticket as Possible 37

Bonus...39

Chapter 1: Wealth Goes to the One with the Timeliest Information

1.1 Why Sell Information Online?

The Internet! The World Wide Web! The Information Super Highway! There is a very good reason why it is call the information super highway. That reason is because that is exactly what it is.

There are, of course, some 'slow lanes' for those who only want to talk to friends and play games but most people now days turn to the Internet for the purpose of getting answers to questions about everything you can imagine and a few things you would never want to try to imagine.

They buy things and sell things…both require information. They search for ways to make money using their computers…for that they REALLY need information.

They search for information about the illnesses they or their family face or they research projects for work or school. Information is THE Internet commodity that almost everybody with a computer wants.

There is a lot of information online that costs nothing above the cost of the Internet connection but timely, relevant, vital information is one thing that people eagerly take out their credit cards to buy.

People will buy information that they can't get free and, the strange thing is, they will also buy information that is readily available on the Internet free of charge if it is packaged in a way that makes it easy to read and understand.

Information is the ultimate commodity and wealth goes to those there first with the timeliest information!

For those looking for a way to earn a living while sitting in front of their computers in their own homes, I recommend selling information. Information is a beautiful thing.

It requires no warehouse space and, unless it is in the form of a CD or DVD, it requires no shipping or handling either.

The one thing that people will gladly pay for is information that is timely, relevant and helps them solve a problem, feel better or look better.

1.2 The Single Most Important Kind of Information You Should Sell

Getting aboard the information gravy train is not as easy as it sounds but it will be well worth the effort it takes. Internet surfers have one thing in common.

They are almost always looking for information that will help them look better, feel better, make more money, answer their questions or solve their problems.

The common denominator of all informational products is 'need'.

Different people, of course, are looking for different information. The quest for information runs the gauntlet and covers every topic that can be imagined. The

thing that doesn't change is that the information needs to be right up-to-date and relevant.

It is possible to create and sell an informational product that is filled with information that is actually available for free on the Internet. I said possible...not easy.

The information that can be found on any given subject on the Internet isn't all relevant or timely. When creating such an informational product, a great many pages of old and out dated information must be sorted through and then discarded.

Only relevant and timely information should be included in any informational product that is sold as such on the Internet.

People in general are much more likely to pull out their credit cards and fill in information to buy an informational product that they believe will help them in some way than they will to buy any other kind of thing sold on the Internet today.

People want and need information and they are willing, even eager, to pay for that information but only if it is relevant and timely.

The single most important kind of information you should sell on the Internet, is that which is relevant and timely no matter what the subject may be.

1.3 A Variety of Information Types You Can Sell Online

Information can be prepared and sold in at least three different kinds of products.

It can be in the form of the written word (E-Books), it can be in the form of an online audio or a CD or tape or it can be in the form of a video online or on DVD.

It is a well known fact that people learn best in different ways. Some people need only read information and it is clear to them. Other people learn best when they hear the information....just reading information doesn't do it for them.

Yet other people need to see the information presented for them to comprehend and grasp the information.

The type of information being presented also lends itself best to either the written word, and audio tape or CD or a video presentation. There are some things, for example, that just the written word can't convey adequately.

Some 'how-to' information will just simply require video and some things like motivational speakers are best presented on audio tape or CD's.

Let's discuss the three different types of informational products that you might consider.

1. The written word (E-Books): This type of informational product is by far the easiest and least expensive to produce. This medium lends itself well to many topics and can even be used for some 'how-to' informational products and motivational products. A well written E-Book that is filled with timely and relevant information sells well on the Internet. E-Books can be sold at a much smaller price to the consumer than other kinds of products because there are no direct production costs....the investment is usually entirely the time of the author of such products. The only tools required to produce an E-Book is a program like MS Word and a PDF converter.

2. The audio product: The audio informational product requires all of the same research that an E-Book requires but then it also requires production and distribution investment, as well. The good news is that with today's computers and the software available, recording audio is a fairly simple

thing to do and the quality is as good, or almost as good, as recordings made in sound studios. Audio informational products are generally used for producing such informational products as those produced for motivation purposes, marketing, finance, and business.

Production, shipping and handling is usually supplied by a fulfillment center. There are many such companies.

3. The video informational product: This is the most difficult and usually the most expensive to produce informational product on the market today.

It is also the most effective for many topics. Unless you have the capability to make the video yourself, you will have to hire a videographer or at the very least you will have to buy or rent video equipment. However, there are some informational topics that just cannot be created in any other way, i.e. action oriented themes like sports, dancing, learning to play a musical instrument, etc. A fulfillment center must be hired in order to mass produce a DVD and distribute it. Of course, some video products can be available only online which eliminates the need for a fulfillment center.

When you are choosing the type of informational product you will produce, take into consideration the cost but also consider the best way to present the information to your customers.

The E-Book can be used for many, maybe even most, topics. It is the least expensive to produce.

The audio product lends itself well to such topics as motivation, marketing, finance, and business.

Info Product Creation Strategies - 6

The video product must be used for producing action oriented topics like sports, dancing, learning to play a musical instrument, etc.

Chapter 2: First Step to Info Product Creation Strategies

2.1 Begin Your Info Product Creation Journey with the End in Mind

In order to create a successful informational product, whether that product is in the form of an E-Book or on audio or video, the creator must begin with the end, rather than the beginning, in mind.

The purpose of all informational products is to make the purchasers of the product feel better, look better, make more money, have more fun, learn something they want to know or solve a problem.

In other words, the object of every informational product is to help those who purchase it in some way that is important to them but the final objective of the creator of an informational product is to sell it to a large pool of hungry prospects that are looking forward to buying the information on a certain topic.

Creating an informational product of any kind is an exciting prospect and the journey between having a good idea and seeing a finished product is marked by many ups and downs, successes and failures, good days and bad.

It's easy to lose sight of the main objective during the creation process. That main objective for the creator of every informational product no matter what the subject is to sell the product when it is completed.

You need customers... customers who are eagerly awaiting your informational product.

Before you even begin creating your informational product, you need to begin seeking that pool of potential buyers by contacting owners of lists that would be most interested and suggesting joint ventures or even partnerships for your product.

Remember this: Creating your informational product and making it as good as you can possibly make it is important...vital, even, but selling the product is what will produce the income you need and pay you for all of the time and effort that you will be putting into creating the product in the first place.

2.2 The Art of Creating Information on Demand

There is so much misinformation out there about how to go about choosing the topic of an informational product and creating an information on demand product for which there will be a large pool of customers eager, ready, willing and able to buy that product.

There are many long articles and dissertations on the Internet that will tell you that the way to choose a topic for an informational product is to simply type a few words into a search engine and see how many hits you get. Nothing could be further from the truth. You might go to Google and type in 'crab'.

You might even go to the Overture Search Tool and type in 'crab'. You will get pages and pages of hits but that doesn't mean that anybody is willing to buy an informational product about crabs.

The only thing it means is that there is a lot of information on the Internet about crabs. If you trusted this search and acted on the fact that you got a lot of hits, you will work hard at creating an informational product for which there will be no market and no buyers.

You will have invested many hours of research that you will never make the first penny on. You will know a lot about crabs but that won't buy milk for the baby.

There are effective ways to search out topics to create information on demand products for, though. They aren't as easy or as quick as using a search engine of the Overture Search Tool but they are a lot more effective.

One such way is to visit online forums. It isn't necessary to join the forums or participate in them. Most forums are public and you can read the posts and discover the hot topics of conversation.

When you see a recurring theme, you may have found the topic of your next information on demand product.

Of course, it doesn't hurt to join the forum and participate in the conversation.

This will give you the opportunity to ask questions and gather information.

Visiting blogs can be useful in finding the topic of your next information on demand product, as well. You can fairly quickly see what is on the minds of those who are posting to blogs.

It's easy to spot controversy...controversy is profitable. You might even find topics for two informational products...one expounding the strong points of each side of a hot topic issue.

Yet another place to look for topics of on-demand informational products in by subscribing to E-zines. Note what kinds of informational products the publishers of these E-zines are promoting.

You will get emails from the publishers of the E-zines and you will be able to determine what products they are promoting. If several publishers are promoting the same kind of product then you can bet its hot.

Hard copy newspapers and magazines are another place to search for topics. It's hard to believe but people who live and die by the Internet do still subscribe to and read them.

Particularly note the letters to the editor section and the business and entertainment sections of these publications.

Note the subject matter being aired on Network television. Pay particular attention to the news-magazine programs. Networks have deep pockets and they pay people a lot of money to figure out what subjects the public will be most interested in.

You need to know what people are talking about and what they are most urgent concerns are. These are the things that determine what on-demand informational products will have a ready made market for your product.

2.3 Info Product Creation Success Factors

The creation of an informational product that will be successful depends on several factors. Just blindly pulling a topic out of thin air will almost certainly guarantee failure rather than success.

The first thing that you must to is to ascertain that there is a demand for the informational product that you plan to create. If there isn't a demand, then there really isn't any point in putting forth the time and effort required to create it.

The best way to check that there is, in fact, a demand for the product is to visit forums and blogs that relate to the product you are planning. Check E-zines and hard copy newspapers and magazines to be sure that people are interested in or need the product.

When checking sources like online forums and blogs, E-zines, and hard copy magazines and newspapers, you don't want to only occasionally see a mention of the desire for the informational product that you are considering creating.

The subject covered in the product needs to have mass appeal at least to a particular market or niche.

The next thing to determine is people would be willing to actually pay for the information that will be contained in the informational product that you are considering.

If the only information you can provide is readily available, you may not have many takers, although it is true that some people will, most won't.

The information that you are planning to publish, needs to be timely and relevant...it must be cutting edge information, in order for people to be willing to pay you for it.

Finally, the information that you are considering creating an informational product from must make people feel better, look better, help them make more money, have fun, or solve a problem that they have. If it doesn't do any of the above, you should look for a different topic.

Chapter 3: Creating Info Products on the Fly!

3.1 Types of Info Products You Can Create

Informational products come in three specific forms. There are the written variety (E-Books), audio tapes or CD's and there are video products that are either in the form of a DVD or available on the Internet.

The topics of informational products are as varied as the people who buy them.

There are informational products sold everyday on every subject you can possibly imagine and probably on a lot of subjects you would rather never imagine.

People buy information. Information is a commodity that is valued in every industrialized society on the planet.

No matter what vehicle you choose to use to present your informational product (E-Book, audio or video), topics fall into general categories and the vehicle you choose needs to be the best one to present your information to your audience.

One type of informational product that is probably the very most popular is the how-to product. If you know how to do anything at all, there are people out there who want to know how to do it, as well.

People are interesting in everything from building bird houses to scuba diving to starting their own Internet business and they are willing to pay for the information about how to do the thing they desire to learn.

An E-Book works well for teaching many how-to-do things but if the subject being taught requires learning an action (sports, dancing, or playing a musical instrument for example) then a video is the better choice.

Inspirational or motivational information products are good sellers on the Internet.

Products that are filled with success stories and case studies give people hope...and hope is in demand every where.

Products that give up-to-date information about chronic diseases are always in demand.

Every day people are diagnosed with some kind of disease they have no information about and they want to know everything they can learn about it and they want to hear how other people deal with it.

Choose a topic that will help people solve a problem or make their lives better in some way and you will have a winning informational product for which there will be a ready made market.

3.2 Churning Out In-Demand Info Products in a Zap

The fact of the matter is that no matter how long it takes you to create an informational product, you aren't going to make a red dime on it until it is sold.

You might spend months or years creating a product but no matter how wonderful it is, you aren't going to be able to pay the rent or buy the groceries until you sell the product.

So even if you have a pet project that is going to take awhile to get to market, it might serve you well to figure out how to zap up products that can be gotten to market quickly and efficiently....and there are ways to do that very thing.

The first thing that you DO need to worry about is the topic of this informational product that you are planning to zap up in a hurry. It needs to cover subject matter that is of vital interest to a large segment of the buying public.

The information contained in it must be easily located (remember that you are doing this in a very short period of time) and the information needs to also be easy to access.

The term 'information' is being used loosely here. Information can mean a lot of things...interviews with well known people, for example, is information.

The first thing that you DON'T need to worry about is how you are going to get this information written or produced.

You don't have to do everything yourself. Work can be outsourced...successful Internet marketers outsource work every day.

If you have a topic and a brief outline of the subject matter you want to have covered, there are ghost writers that can produce an E-Book in a few days.

There are companies that specialize in producing audio and video products and there are programmers that can get these products online in a matter of hours.

Sources for informational products that can be zapped up practically overnight are available in the public domain. This information if there and free for the taking.

Interviews with people who were once headliners but have fallen off the front page are big sellers in the informational product market. As a rule, these people are eager to be heard and usually grant interviews without much hassle.

People who were in the headlines always have stories to tell and they are more than willing to share experiences and give you insight that can easily be turned into an informational product that will have a large eager-to-buy pool of customers.

Short how-to E-Books about a subject that you are well versed in and that will not require any research are another idea for a quickly assembled informational product.

Since you already know how to do whatever it is...all you have to do is get it written down or get a ghost writer to write it down for you and with no research time invested, you can have an informational product ready to market in almost nothing flat.

It is absolutely true that quality in informational products matters. It doesn't just 'matter', it is vital but it isn't written anywhere that a quality product has to take months or years to develop.

The truth is that once you have a good idea for a topic, you can get from idea to product in two week's time or less. By employing the ideas set forth in this article, you can have not one, but many informational products on the market in a fairly short period of time.

The only way you make money from any informational product is when it is sold!

3.3 The Elements of a Top Quality Info Product

What exactly is the purpose of an informational product other than to impart information? Or, is there one?

Well, yes, there is another objective. It is to impart information and do it in a way that the information is easily and quickly absorbed by the buyer of that information.

The creator of informational products should have respect for the time of the buyer of the product.

Everybody gets the same number of hours in a day and each person considers their alloted share valuable. Wasting a person's time is, in a way, disrespectful.

It isn't written anywhere that an E-Book needs to be forty or fifty pages long. That many pages of single spaced type takes a long time to read and even longer to absorb and put into action.

Most of the time people who buy informational E-Books do so for the purpose of gaining knowledge or solving a problem and they usually want to do either in the shortest period of time possible.

They really don't want to wade through irrelevant information that is there for the sole purpose of making the E-Book fifty pages long.

An E-Book should be only twenty to forty pages long depending upon the information contained in it and sometimes E-Books can be a lot shorter than twenty pages and still be effective.

The whole point of an E-Book is to convey information and do it in as efficient manner as possible. As long as the product offers a solution to a problem, informs the reader or makes his life better in some way, it has done what it was designed to do.

People buy E-Books for the sole purpose of gaining the information in them.

Their time is valuable and you should remember that sometimes people are desperate for information or, at the very least, have a limited amount of time to read and absorb the information in them.

3.4 Branding Your Info Product

Yee Haw! Years ago the way cattle were marked so that they could be identified was by 'branding' them with a symbol that represented their owner.

There was a red hot branding iron involved...OUCH! That method is rarely used now...ear tags are more the norm.

The idea of branding an animal was for the purpose of identification. The idea of 'branding' a product is a little more complicated but the idea is the same.

You recognize many brands of many different products by their logo's, colors and fonts.

Every year, billions of dollars are spent on advertising so that the buying public will recognize a particular brand of a general product.

We have all heard the term 'branding' and 'branding campaign' used in the Internet marketing arena, but what exactly does it mean in that setting?

According to Capcomarketing it means, "An ad campaign that focuses on introducing, re-introducing or enforcing the brand for a particular product or organization.

Branding is one of the most unappreciated aspects of web advertising because so many people focus on click-through rates.

This is unfortunate because studies have shown Internet advertising to be highly successful in building brand awareness." "Interesting', you say, "but how does branding relate to my informational product?" The fact is that every day there are hundreds of E-Books published or offered on the Internet. Branding is one way to make yours stand out from the crowd.

The objective is always to stand out, stand above and be recognized. The purpose of branding your informational product is to establish yourself as a guru...an expert in the field...the 'go-to' guy (or gal).

There are several things that you can do that will help you establish a recognizable brand for your informational products. One such thing is to have a logo made that is yours alone.

Think Coca Cola or Tide! You would recognize those brand logos anywhere. If you are a graphic designer you can, of course, design your own logo.

If you are like most of us, you will need to find a graphic designer to make one for you.

Think of it as a one-time expense that will have value for you forever. Use this logo on all of your informational products and be sure that when it is reproduced the logo will be included in the reproduction.

Another way of branding your informational product is to use your own picture as a part of the work.

This will help to establish you as the guru and any reproduction of the work should include the picture.

Use a slogan often enough that it becomes associated with your informational products.

A slogan needs to be short and to the point. Think of the Wal-Mart slogan...Always low prices...always!" It works for them and a slogan can help you brand your products, as well.

This slogan should be used as a part of your informational product as often as possible.

You can still have no idea how to brand your informational product, the one thing that you can do free of charge and every time is to put your name in the title of your informational product. "John Doe Teaches You How-to Whatever" is an effective way to brand an E-Book or a CD or DVD.

As small Internet business owners, we just don't have those beautiful multi- million advertising budgets that the bug guys have but we can use some of the same tactics that have made them big guys and branding is one of those tactics.

Brand your informational products to help establish yourself as an expert in your field and thereby increase you income.

3.5 Getting Your Product's Digital Cover

"You can't tell a book by its cover" is a phrase that adults repeat to children that tell them not to judge people by how they look... and it is good advice.

However, the cover of a real book is what causes people to purchase that book out in the real world.

Real world books aren't just pages of type...they come wrapped in a cover that is attractive, appealing to the eye and designed to encourage people to buy the book.

E-Books are no different. The E-Book is digital....and it needs an attractive and appealing cover designed to encourage people to buy it that is also digital.

Just a page with a title isn't going to attract many buyers to your E-Book no matter how great the title is or how informative the content.

If you have very deep pockets and money is simply no object, you can hire a graphic designer who can create a digital E-Book cover for you.

On the other hand, if you are like most of us small Internet business owners there is another alternative.

You can buy software that will allow you to create your own E-Book covers. It comes several varieties.

You can buy software that will design E-Book covers that are 2D or 3D. The best of the best of this software is made by Project Storm, in my opinion.

The Project Storm software doesn't require in-depth graphic design capability. It is easy to use and with it you can even do graphic design for others. Graphic design is a rather lucrative enterprise and one that you can tap into with this software.

You invest much time and effort into creating an informational E-Book. It needs a digital cover to make it appealing and attractive to your potential customers.

Chapter 4: Applying the Finishing Touches

4.1 How to Protect the Value of Your Info Product

How much time, effort, energy, blood, sweat and tears do you invest in a digital informational product before it is ready to be introduced into the market place?

Not just a little, that's for sure! Protecting the value of your informational product is certainly the prudent thing to do.

It used to be that the creator of any work had to register it with the Office of Copyright in order for it to be protected.

On March 1, 1989 the United States decided to adhere to the Berne Commission and this is no longer the case. An original work is determined to be copyrighted when it is created.

It is perfectly legal to use the copyright symbol (©), the word, "copyright" or the abbreviation, "Copr" on your E-Books or other informational products and you should.

This serves as notice that your work is, in fact, copyrighted and that you intend to protect it.

In the resource box of your digital informational product, be sure that you include your full name, the year it was created and/or modified and the copyright symbol.

Your contact information, as well as, a link to your website should also be in the resource box.

A statement that gives permission for use of the article or E-Book should include the stipulation that all information in the resource box be included.

You can check to see if your work is being reproduced without your consent or without including your name and information on CopyScape.com.

You can also obtain a free banner that states that the information on your website is copyrighted on the copyscape site.

You work hard and long to produce an informational product whether it is an E- Book, a CD or a DVD. That hard work needs to be protected so that you, and you alone, retain the value of your product.

4.2 Determining Your Info Product's Terms of Use

You and you alone should determine your informational product's terms of use statement.

Your informational product is considered to be an "intellectual work" and it is automatically copyrighted when you have completed it.

It is your decision about how your informational product can be used.

Most of the time the only thing that is needed is a statement saying that the work cannot be used unless it is used in it entirety and that includes all links, copyright information, your full name and your contact information.

If registration on your website is a requirement for purchasing your product, then you should have a privacy statement available to be read.

This statement should assure customers that information they provide in order to download your E-Book will be kept confidential.

Your customers need to be assured that their email addresses will not be shared and that they will not have an inbox full of spam because they bought your product. That is what you give them.

What they give you is a promise that they won't use your product for any purpose other than the purpose it was intended for.

They need to guarantee you that they will not reproduce the product and resell it for their personal gain even if they include all of the information in your resource box. You also need to make any disclaimers that you feel are necessary.

A 'Term's of Use" statement can be many pages long and filled with a lot of legalese or it can be a simple statement that consists of only a few lines such as: "This E-Book is for your personal use only. It is not to be reproduced without the express consent of the owner. The information contain in this E-Book is not to be censored legal or medical advice."

Chapter 5: Entering Your Info Product into the Market War Zone

5.1 How to Strategically Price Your Product

Now that you have your digital informational product complete and ready to be sold, the next question is what to charge for it.

How much should you ask for your work?

That is a hard question to answer but the general rule of thumb is: The more potential customers there are for your product the less you can charge for it and the opposite is true.

The fewer potential customers there are, the more you should charge for it.

Think about how products are priced out in the brick and mortar world. In very exclusive shops, where very exclusive products are sold to only a few well- heeled customers, the prices are high....VERY high.

On the other hand, prices of similar products are priced much lower in department stores and even lower in giant chain stores like Wal-Mart.

The reason that the products are priced lower is because there are a lot more buyers for them and more product will be sold. It is just simple mathematics.

You can sell 10 people an item for $100 each and gross $1000. You can sell 100 people a $10 item and still gross $1000.

The fact is that there are more people who can afford to spend $10 than there people who can afford to spend $100.

There is another consideration to be made when pricing your informational product and that is that it takes the same amount of effort and energy to promote a $10 product as it does to promote a product that sells for $100.

It takes the same amount of time, as well. Your product needs to be priced as high as it can possibly be priced.

The amount of information in the product and how valuable that information is to the customers who will buy the product needs to be considered. Correct pricing is a balancing act.

Have you ever heard the old saying, "You can price yourself right out of the market"?

If an informational product is prices too low, people think it will have little value and not be worth their time or effort to read it.

On the other hand, if an informational product is priced too high, people might really want it but feel like they simply can't afford the price.

Consider the information that is contained in the E-Book or other informational product.

Is it new information that will help to solve a pressing problem for many people or only for a few people?

Is the information contained in the product available elsewhere or is your product the only place this information can be found?

Will it make people look better, feel better, make more money, have fun or solve a problem and is it the kind of information that people would be willing to pay a lot of money for or only a little money for?

Will your informational product appeal to a very large pool of potential customers or only to a few people but be of a great value to those few?

Sometimes, adding on some freebies or bonuses allows you to ask a higher price. Bundling products sometimes allows for higher pricing, as well.

Pricing your informational product is a sticky and tricky problem. Pricing it too low is just as bad as pricing it too high.

If there are similar informational products on the market, you should check their prices and not price yours too far from the center.

Remember this...you can always lower a price but you can never raise a price on the same product so set your price at the highest level you believe that you can get because you will work just as hard for a $10 sale as you will for a $100 sale.

5.2 How to Gather Testimonials for Your Product

Most people like to read testimonials about how good a product is before they buy it. They are particularly interested in what other customers have to say about a product. This holds true for digital informational products, as well.

If you have written a how-to E-Book, testimonials about how others have succeeded by using the information provided in the E-Book are the testimonials of the greatest value you can get to add to your sales letter.

You can waste a lot of time, effort and energy seeking out testimonials by giving away free copies of your E-Book or other digital informational product to E-zine editors and others that you believe could be influential in getting your product noticed.

Not that you shouldn't do so...you should...but you shouldn't expect to get those testimonials right away. Pursue all avenues to get good testimonials as to the value of your informational product but concentrate on getting testimonials from your customers first.

For starters, reserve some space in your sales letter for testimonials from your customers...even if you only have a few customers.

Everybody has to start somewhere and don't expect miracles. You will be sadly disappointed. Your conversion rate might not be earth shaking to begin with.

Ask your customers for feedback. Surprisingly enough, people like to be asked what they think.

They really like for their opinion to be sought after and they will usually give you testimonials if you will only ask and most especially if you have a terrific product.

Testimonials from high-powered, well-known people are great. Get them if you can. Just don't expend too much time and energy seeking them out.

Testimonials from happy customers are of a great value as well and they are a lot easier to get.

5.3 Writing Your Sales Letter

Writing an effective sales letter should probably be considered an art form or maybe it should be included as part of the punishment for white collar crimes.

Writing an effective sales letter is one of the hardest tasks an Internet entrepreneur has to face and those who create digital informational products are not exempt.

A sales letter is required so you may as well write a great one.

There are thousands...maybe millions of sales letters that go out everyday out in the brick and mortar world and probably twice that many in cyber space.

Think of all the things that are for sale in the world and you can bet that there is a sales letter attached to most of them.

So, how, in Heaven's name, are you supposed to write a sales letter that will stand out in that kind of crowd?

A sales letter is only one page long...so you only get the one shot. Make it count!

Here are a few ideas that might help: 1. Put yourself in your customer's shoes. Pretend for a minute that you are the customer that is being asked to buy the digital informational product that you are, in reality, trying to sell. Ask yourself why you would want to buy this product. Ask yourself what this product could do that would make you look better, feel better, make more money, have more fun, give you some kind of vital information that you desperately need or

solve a pressing problem. Just look at what you are selling through the eyes of the buyer.

2. The headline is all important. You have got to grab the readers attention in the first few words of your sales letter or it is a lost cause. The headline must grab and hold the readers attention from the get-go. It needs to be short, sweet and directly to the point and make them continue reading.

3. Get your words and thoughts organized. A sales letter basically has three parts. There is the introduction, the sales pitch and the conclusion.

The introduction is used to tell the reader why you are contacting them.

The sales pitch is the body of the letter. In it you tell them about the product and how it will make their lives better in some way. The conclusion is used to give them irrefutable reasons why they should purchase your product and the means to do so.

4. Now you have a basic sales letter but you aren't through yet. It needs to be fine tuned. Now check to see that you have done the following things well: Is your letter written in a conversational style rather than in a formal business way? People do not like to be spoken to in formal terms. They prefer and respond to a friendly and conversational tone much easier.

Are the sentences in your letter short? Long rambling sentences are confusing to a reader. You will find that the more conversational the tone of your sales letter is, the sentences just naturally become shorter.

How many paragraphs are there in your letter? Several short paragraphs are preferable to 2 or 3 long ones.

Have you used spell check and ascertained that the letter is grammatically correct in every way? Misspelled words and grammatical errors will make you sound....well....there isn't another word....DUMB!

By following these instructions, you should be able to write an effective sales letter.

Give your potential customers a good sales pitch and you will be on your way to selling your informational product.

5.4 Don't Get into Business without Back-End Products!

The quickest way out of the business of selling informational products on the Internet is to adopt a "take the money and run" attitude.

Getting customers to buy informational products isn't easy.

A customer is valuable and should be treasured above all else.

Out of every hundred people who visit your website and consider buying your E- Book or other informational product, you will be doing very well indeed if you make 3 sales.

Those are just the cold hard facts of selling digital informational products....or any other kind of product on the Internet.

Getting a first-time customer isn't easy. When you get one you need to make sure that you keep him, keep him happy and make him want to buy from you again and again.

You do that by having excellent customer service, staying in contact with you customers through newsletters and emails and by having great back-end products to offer him.

Remember this: it is much easier to sell to and existing customer than it is to get a new customer.

You should include an offer for a back-end product with the delivery of the first sale to a customer. Let them know right away that you have other products to sell.

If they are happy with the first product, they will be much more likely to buy the back-end products as well.

In digital products such as E-Books, the offer of the back-end products needs to be included in the original E-Book...the offers should be made a part of the E- Book itself.

Including membership in a 'members only' forum or blog where buyers can discuss the product is a great idea. It also gives you a place to continue to promote your back-end products.

Make your customers believe in you, your expertise and your products and your business can only grow larger over time. Don't take the money and run....that strategy doesn't work.

Chapter 6: In Closing

6.1 A Crash Course Guide on Marketing to Your Prospects

The Internet is known as the "Information Super Highway". If it is a super highway, digital informational products are the on-ramps for budding Internet entrepreneurs. Sadly, they can also be the off-ramps.

A great product can put you into the fast lane but a really lousy product can cause the wheels to come off and you'll be off on the next exit.

Digital informational products can come in different forms....E-Books, audio tapes and CD's and video or any combination of these mediums.

The creation of any kind of informational digital product takes many hours of time and untold effort.

Not only that....there are thousands of E-Books and other informational products created everyday, sales letters are written, products are submitted to experts for review, E-zine publishers are inundated with requests for publication of products.

In other words...the competition is stiff...and that is a huge understatement.

First and foremost the subject of an informational product must have mass appeal.

A product that covers a subject that would only be of interest to three people on the planet (and two of them live on a mountain top in Peru) isn't going to do very well no matter how well it is marketed.

Oh....and it has to have a killer title!

Second...the product must be top quality. There can't be any rough patches or pot holes in an informational product. All of the included links must work. The audio must play and the video must be sharp.

It must, of course, have every word spelled correctly and used correctly...spelling and grammar count!

No matter how great the information contained in a product is, if the links don't work, there are problems with audio or video or the product is filled with misspelled words and grammatical errors, it isn't going to fly.

When the above criteria have been met, the product is then ready to be marketed.

There are several ways that an informational product can be presented to the buying public.

Depending upon the subject and the projected available pool of potential customers, it can be marketed as a stand-alone product.

If the informational product is to be marketed as a stand-alone product it should probably contain different types of media...i.e. text, html, graphics, animation and/or video.

Using a compiler, the media is inserted and the E-Book is produced in a 'pdf' or 'exe' file.

It can be easily downloaded from any website. The compiler allows affiliates to insert their links and URL as a distributor of the product.

The creator of the informational product, of course, does maintain complete control over what information can be changed or inserted into the work.

If, on the other hand, the informational product is to be used as a marketing tool to promote a website or other products and is not a stand-alone product in and of itself, the marketing approach is a bit different.

In this case, the informational product is given away free for the purpose of promoting a larger enterprise.

When an E-Book is to be used in this manner, it is of the utmost importance that the resource box contain copyright information, links to the larger enterprise and contact information.

They can be submitted to E-zine publishers to be used for free in there publications and they can be listed in directories for other website owners to use as long as all of the creator's information and all of the links contained in the product remain unchanged.

Marketing of informational products can be tricky and sticky but it doesn't have to be. If the product is really top drawer and has mass appeal, marketing it is a lot easier.

6.2 School of Thought: Go as High-Ticket as Possible

Producing an informational product (i.e. E-Book, audio or video) takes time.

Some products take more time to create than others, of course but it takes the same amount of time, effort and energy to market an informational product that sells for $10 as it does to market one that costs $100.

So, stating the obvious, you should price your informational product as high as possible.

You may not sell as many units if you price it higher but you will gross the same amount of money. It's basically simply mathematics. If you sell 100 units at $10 you gross $1000. If you sell 10 units at $100, you still gross $1000.

People equate the price of an item with the value or importance of that item. If an informational product is priced too low, people will see it as having little value.

If the same product is priced too high, they may want it but simply not feel like they can afford to buy it.

Just the right pricing for any product is a difficult number to arrive at but the rule of thumb is to price it as high as you possibly can.

The information contained in the product will, of course, helps to determine the price that should be charged for it.

It is a known fact that people are willing to pay top dollar for informational products that will make the look better, feel better, make more money, have more fun, learn how to do something that is important to them or solve an immediate and pressing problem.

They will pay more money for information that they cannot get other places than they will pay for information that is readily available on the Internet and can be accessed with a little effort.

The bottom line here is that you should set the price for your informational product as high as possible.

Bonus

Get Related Materials

from Our Free Library

Instant Access – Join Here

Click or type into your browser:

http://livesensical.com/go/byob/

www.ingramcontent.com/pod-product-compliance
Lightning Source LLC
Chambersburg PA
CBHW021850170526
45157CB00006B/2382